DAVID

DEVELOPING A HEART FOR GOD

JACK
KUHATSCHEK

12 STUDIES
FOR INDIVIDUALS
OR GROUPS

Life
Builder
Study

INTER-VARSITY PRESS
36 Causton Street, London SW1P 4ST, England
Email: ivp@ivpbooks.com
Website: www.ivpbooks.com

Originally published in the United States of America in the LifeGuide® Bible Studies series in 1990 by InterVarsity Press, Downers Grove, Illinois
Second edition published 2001
First published in Great Britain by Scripture Union in 2001
Second edition published 2016
This edition published in Great Britain by Inter-Varsity Press 2018

British Library Cataloguing-in-Publication Data
A catalogue record for this book is available from the British Library.

ISBN: 978–1–78359–791–8

Printed and bound in Great Britain by Clays Ltd, Elcograf S.p.A.

Contents

Getting the Most Out of *David*

When I was a child my hero was Superman. Like him, I wanted to be faster than a speeding bullet, able to leap tall buildings in a single bound and able to bend steel in my bare hands. Using a bath towel for my cape, I flew around the house, performing imaginary feats of strength and courage.

As I grew up, however, I discovered that Superman was not the best kind of hero. I found it impossible to be like him, no matter how hard I tried. Bullets simply wouldn't bounce off me and neither would harsh words, fears, disappointments, illnesses or a hundred other weaknesses that are common to a frail, fallen humanity.

Bullets didn't bounce off David either. As I read about his life, I am astonished at how open and vulnerable he was. He records his weaknesses and struggles for all the world to read: "I am worn out from groaning; all night long I flood my bed with weeping and drench my couch with tears. My eyes grow weak with sorrow; they fail me because of all my foes." "I know my transgressions, and my sin is always before me. Against you, you only, have I sinned and done what is evil in your sight" (Psalm 6:6-7; 51:3-4).

Yet in spite of all his weaknesses, fears, doubts and sins, David was also a man of faith. His life illustrates a tenacious trust in God and an intense desire to know him: "The LORD is my light and my salvation—whom shall I fear? The LORD is the stronghold of my life—of whom shall I be afraid?" "One thing I ask of the LORD, this is what I seek: that I may dwell in the house of the LORD, . . . to seek him in his temple" (Psalm 27:1, 4). Because of these qualities, God was able to use David mightily, molding and shaping him into a man after his own heart.

I believe we need this kind of three-dimensional role model today—someone who allows us to be fully human, yet who inspires us to look beyond our weaknesses and frailties to the living God. This study guide allows us to observe David from the beginning of his career to the end of his life. It doesn't cover every detail but rather selects key events that reveal the multifaceted character of this remarkable man. Each study also focuses on the real hero of every biblical narrative—the Lord himself.

David's life extended from around 1040 to 970 B.C. Second Samuel 5 records that "David was thirty years old when he became king, and he reigned forty years. In Hebron he reigned over Judah seven years and six months, and in Jerusalem he reigned over all Israel and Judah thirty-three years" (vv. 4, 5). The biblical writers view David as the greatest of Israel's kings and the one through whom the ultimate king, the Messiah, eventually came (see Matthew 1:1; Luke 3:31).

It is my prayer that as you study the life of David, you too will develop a passionate heart for God.

Suggestions for Individual Study

1. As you begin each study, pray that God will speak to you through his Word.

2. Read the introduction to the study and respond to the personal reflection question or exercise. This is designed to help you focus on God and on the theme of the study.

3. Each study deals with a particular passage—so that you can delve into the author's meaning in that context. Read and reread the passage to be studied. The questions are written using the language of the New International Version, so you may wish to use that version of the Bible. The New Revised Standard Version is also recommended.

4. This is an inductive Bible study, designed to help you discover for yourself what Scripture is saying. The study includes three types of questions. *Observation* questions ask about the basic facts: who, what, when, where and how. *Interpretation* questions delve into the meaning of the passage. *Application* questions help you discover the implications of the text for growing in Christ. These three keys unlock the treasures of Scripture.

Write your answers to the questions in the spaces provided or in a personal journal. Writing can bring clarity and deeper understanding of yourself and of God's Word.

5. It might be good to have a Bible dictionary handy. Use it to look up any unfamiliar words, names or places.

6. Use the prayer suggestion to guide you in thanking God for what you have learned and to pray about the applications that have come to mind.

7. You may want to go on to the suggestion under "Now or Later," or you may want to use that idea for your next study.

Suggestions for Members of a Group Study

1. Come to the study prepared. Follow the suggestions for individual study mentioned above. You will find that careful preparation will greatly enrich your time spent in group discussion.

2. Be willing to participate in the discussion. The leader of your group will not be lecturing. Instead, he or she will be encouraging the members of the group to discuss what they have learned. The leader will be asking the questions that are found in this guide.

3. Stick to the topic being discussed. Your answers should be based on the verses which are the focus of the discussion and not on outside authorities such as commentaries or speakers. These studies focus on a particular passage of Scripture. Only rarely should you refer to other portions of the Bible. This allows for everyone to participate in in-depth study on equal ground.

4. Be sensitive to the other members of the group. Listen attentively when they describe what they have learned. You may be surprised by their insights! Each question assumes a variety of answers. Many questions do not have "right" answers, particularly questions that aim at meaning or application. Instead the questions push us to explore the passage more thoroughly.

When possible, link what you say to the comments of others. Also, be affirming whenever you can. This will encourage some of the more hesitant members of the group to participate.

5. Be careful not to dominate the discussion. We are sometimes so eager to express our thoughts that we leave too little opportunity for others to respond. By all means participate! But allow others to also.

6. Expect God to teach you through the passage being discussed and through the other members of the group. Pray that you will have an enjoyable and profitable time together, but also that as a result of the study you will find ways that you can take action individually and/or as a group.

7. Remember that anything said in the group is considered confidential and should not be discussed outside the group unless specific permission is given to do so.

8. If you are the group leader, you will find additional suggestions at the back of the guide.

1

The Lord Looks at the Heart

1 Samuel 16:1-13

In the movie *Twins* some genetic engineers combine the genes from several of the best men they can find—a brilliant scientist, a powerful athlete, a talented musician, a great artist, and a tall and incredibly handsome hunk. They implant these super genes into a mother's womb. But by accident, they also implant all of the leftover genetic "junk." Then nine months later out pops the ideal (according to our culture) baby, who grows up to be the ideal man: Arnold Schwarzenegger. But to everyone's surprise a second baby also pops out—the embodiment of everything our culture says you don't want to be as a baby or a man—Danny DeVito!

The implied message of the movie is that if you wanted to pick someone to be CEO of your company or the quarterback for your team or the pastor of your church—or whatever—you'd pick an Arnold Schwarzenegger every time because he is tall, handsome, powerful and intelligent. But the *last* person you would ever pick would be Danny DeVito because he is short, weak and unattractive.

GROUP DISCUSSION. How does a person's appearance affect your initial opinion of him or her?

PERSONAL REFLECTION. In what ways do you try to impress people with your outward appearance?

Israel's first king, Saul, was the ideal candidate—tall, handsome and impressive. Unfortunately, he was also foolish and disobedient. As Israel's second king is chosen, the Lord rejects worldly standards of leadership and selects David, a man after his own heart. *Read 1 Samuel 16:1-13.*

1. What evidence is there in this passage that Samuel is having difficulty letting go of Saul?

2. What specific instructions does the Lord give Samuel for anointing a new king (vv. 1-3)?

3. Why does Samuel suppose that Eliab is the Lord's anointed (vv. 6-7; see 17:13)?

4. According to verse 7, how does God's judgment differ from ours?

5. The Lord tells Samuel, "Man looks at the outward appearance" (v. 7). What sorts of "outward" things do we tend to look at in people?

6. How does our culture reinforce our emphasis on appearance?

7. Why are outward qualities an unreliable way to judge a person?

8. If you had been given the job of finding the next king of Israel, why would David have been an unlikely choice?

In what sense was he also a good choice (see v. 18)?

9. Why do you think the Lord has Samuel look at each of Jesse's sons before revealing that he has chosen David (vv. 6-12)?

10. When the Lord looks at our hearts, what specific qualities do you think he values most? Explain.

Take time to pray, asking the Lord to develop those qualities within you.

Now or Later

George Barna writes, "In the past two decades Americans have been burned by leaders who oozed charisma and flashed world-class rhetorical skills but whose underlying character was debatable, at best." (*The Barna Report* [Nashville, Tenn.: Thomas Nelson, 1998] p. 5). In what ways can we look beyond deceptive appearance and discern a person's true character?

2

The Battle
Is the Lord's

The Bear is a story about an orphaned cub that is adopted by a giant Kodiak bear. The little bear copies everything he sees the big bear doing. He learns to eat honey from a beehive just like the big bear. He learns to fish from a mountain stream. And he learns to scratch his back—up and down and side to side—on a tree trunk just like the big bear.

Then one day, while the little bear is all alone playing in a field, a mountain lion begins to chase him. The bear runs across an open, rocky field and crosses a river. But with a splash and two leaps the mountain lion stands face to face with the baby bear and shows his teeth. He swipes at the bear's face with his claws and draws blood. He swipes again and makes another gash—and your heart breaks as you realize that the little bear is about to die.

But in a desperate attempt, the little bear begins to do what he's seen the big bear do—he stands on all fours, raises up the muscles in his back and begins to growl as fiercely as he can in his baby-bear voice. Suddenly, and surprisingly, a look of fear appears in the mountain lion's eyes. He backs up, turns and runs away while the baby bear continues to growl behind him. Then the camera pans back, and you see what you couldn't see before—although the lion could see it.

About twenty feet behind the growling baby bear the giant Kodiak bear is standing on his hind legs with his arms outstretched, roaring a terrifying growl.

There are many times in life when we face frightening situations like the mountain lion in the story. They may include a job change or a new and challenging ministry or even a life-threatening illness. How do we respond to situations that seem intimidating, overwhelming or even terrifying?

GROUP DISCUSSION. When you are faced with a challenge that seems beyond your abilities, how do you tend to respond?

PERSONAL REFLECTION. What situation are you currently facing that seems overwhelming?

In this passage David doesn't face a mountain lion, but he does face a mountain of a man named Goliath. *Read 1 Samuel 17.*

---

1. Humanly speaking, why were the Israelites justly terrified of Goliath (vv. 1-11)?

---

2. Spiritually speaking, what had the Israelites forgotten about God's covenant promises (see Deuteronomy 20:1-4)?

---

3. As David reaches the army camp, what does he learn about their situation (vv. 12-27)?

4. Why do you think David's brother is so harsh with him (vv. 28-30)?

5. From a human standpoint, why was David an unlikely choice as the champion of Israel (vv. 15, 33, 38-40)?

What risk was Saul taking in allowing David to fight Goliath (vv. 8-9)?

6. Normally, we select people who are humanly qualified to do a job. Likewise, we normally take on responsibilities for which we feel qualified. Does faith remove the need for human qualifications? Why or why not?

When is it proper to trust God to overcome our deficiencies?

7. David is confident that he can defeat Goliath (vv. 34-37). Is this faith or merely youthful bravado? Explain.

8. How can previous spiritual victories encourage us when facing future battles?

9. What impresses you about the conversation and battle between David and Goliath (vv. 41-49)?

10. What "Goliaths" are you currently facing—either at work or home or in your personal life?

11. How can David's experience give you hope and courage as you face those battles?

Take time now to thank God for his powerful presence in your life.

Now or Later

One of the myths of our culture is "if you set your mind to it, you can do anything." The heroes of that myth are self-made men and women, those who climb from obscurity to fame through sheer willpower and determination. The message is clear: victory goes to the strong, and the spoils of victory to those who are powerful.

First Samuel 17 presents a very different picture: "All those gathered here will know that it is not by sword or spear that the LORD saves; for the battle is the LORD's, and he will give all of you into our hands" (v. 47). In this chapter how does David confront not only Goliath but also our myths of human adequacy?

3

True Friendship

1 Samuel 20:1-17, 30-42

When I was growing up, I had a friend named David Miller. David and I met in primary school. In the third grade we were in Cub Scouts together. In the fourth grade we had the same girlfriend. In sixth and seventh grade we went to camp together. Our relationship continued through high school, then we lost touch with each other, and later I moved to another city.

After many years, I went home for a visit and decided to stop by and see David. He was living in the same house—now with his wife and children. After the initial shock and joy at seeing each other, he invited me in. As I went inside, I felt as though I were stepping back in time. All the childhood memories associated with his house flooded back into my mind. What good friends we'd been!

GROUP DISCUSSION. What qualities do you appreciate most in a friend, and why?

PERSONAL REFLECTION. Think of someone you consider a very close friend. How has that person shown you love and faithfulness?

In this study we will explore the strong relationship between David and Jonathan. They help us see and appreciate the qualities of true friendship. *Read 1 Samuel 18:1-4 and 20:1-17.*

1. What impresses you about Jonathan's and David's love for each other?

2. How does their love express itself in their commitment to each other?

3. What kinds of mutual commitments can strengthen our friendships with those we love?

4. *Read 1 Samuel 20:30-42; 2 Samuel 1:25-27.* How does Jonathan's experience with Saul demonstrate some of the cost of friendship?

5. In what other ways can friendship be costly?

6. What do we learn about the level of intimacy between Jonathan and David (1 Samuel 20:41-42; 2 Samuel 1:25-27)?

7. Do you think it is more difficult for women or for men to achieve that kind of intimacy in friendship? Explain.

8. What factors enhance or inhibit intimacy in a relationship?

9. Think of your closest friend. If you could pick one area in which you'd like your friendship to be more like Jonathan and David's, what would it be?

What specific steps can you take to achieve that goal?

Ask the Lord to help you be more like David and Jonathan in your relationships with others.

Now or Later

George Gallup Jr. writes, "We are physically detached from each other. We change places of residence frequently. One survey revealed that seven in ten do not know their neighbors. As many as one-third of Americans admit to frequent periods of loneliness, which is a key factor in the high suicide rate among the elderly" (*Emerging Trends*, Princeton Religious Research Center, March 1997). Why are friendships not just a luxury but a necessity in life?

4

A Matter of Conscience

1 Samuel 24

How do we determine God's will? Do we look to circumstances? the counsel of friends? the words of Scripture?

On April 17, 1521, Martin Luther appeared before the Holy Roman Emperor in order, he thought, to defend his Protestant beliefs. Instead, he was shown all of his writings and asked whether he still believed their contents. Luther asked "for time to think, in order to satisfactorily answer the question without violence to the divine Word and danger to my soul." The next day he stood before the Emperor and uttered the famous words, "Unless I am convinced by the testimony of the Scriptures or by clear reason . . . I am bound by the Scriptures I have quoted, and my conscience is captive to the Word of God. I cannot and will not retract anything, since it is neither safe nor right to go against conscience. I cannot do otherwise. Here I stand. May God help me, Amen."*

GROUP DISCUSSION. How do you determine whether God is leading you to do something?

PERSONAL REFLECTION. In what ways has God given you clear guidance in the past?

In 1 Samuel 24 everything seems to indicate that David should kill Saul and take his place on the throne of Israel. Yet David rejects conventional wisdom and uses a different method for deciding what is right. His attitude should cause us to reexamine our own notions about guidance. *Read 1 Samuel 24.*

1. What feelings and struggles do you think David experienced in this passage?

2. What factors might have convinced David that it was God's will for him to kill Saul (vv. 1-4)?

3. We often rely on circumstances and the counsel of friends when making important decisions. To what extent are these reliable guides?

4. What additional factors convince David that he should not mistreat Saul in any way (vv. 5-7)?

5. Is it ever right to go against conscience in a small area for the sake of a supposedly greater good? Explain.

6. Why do you think David places such importance on respecting the Lord's anointed (vv. 6, 10)?

7. What arguments does David use to convince Saul of his innocence (vv. 8-15)?

8. Describe how Saul responds to David's words (vv. 16-22).

What do David's actions force Saul to conclude about David?

9. David could have killed Saul and seized the throne of Israel. Instead, he relies on God both to avenge him and to establish him as king. Although the result would appear to be the same in both cases, how would it be different?

---

10. How can we know when to take matters into our own hands and when to leave them in God's hands?

---

11. In what area do you need God's guidance?

Ask God for the wisdom to know what is right and the grace to follow his leading.

Now or Later

James writes, "If any of you lacks wisdom, he should ask God, who gives generously to all without finding fault, and it will be given to him" (James 1:5). How does this promise encourage you in a complex and confusing world?

The New Dictionary of the Christian Church, ed. J. D. Douglas (Grand Rapids, Mich., Zondervan, 1974), p. 1062.

5

Secure in the Lord

1 Samuel 25

At one time or another you have probably found yourself saying—or thinking, "I'll get you for this!" "You'll be sorry you ever treated me that way!" "You'll wish you had never been born!" When people mistreat us, we instinctively want revenge. We want to get even, to show them how it feels.

GROUP DISCUSSION. Someone once dumped a large load of garbage on a man's private property. While looking through the garbage, the man found the offender's name and address on an envelope. He quickly loaded up the garbage, drove to the person's house, and dumped the mess in his front yard. Do you think the man's actions were justified or not? Explain.

PERSONAL REFLECTION. When have you been tempted to get even with someone?

In 1 Samuel 25 David is insulted by a man named Nabal. David's response gives us both a positive and negative example of how we should respond to those who mistreat us. *Read 1 Samuel 25.*

---

1. Why do you think the events in this chapter are deliberately sandwiched between two accounts where David had a chance to kill Saul?

2. What does the author tell us about the two new characters in this drama (vv. 2-3)?

3. Why is David so offended by Nabal's response to his request (vv. 4-13, 21-22)?

4. Even if David's offense is justified, how would you evaluate his plan to get even with Nabal (vv. 13, 34)?

5. What methods do we sometimes use to "get even" with those who mistreat us?

6. What impresses you about Abigail's response when she finds out what has happened (vv. 14-32)?

7. How is David's relationship with Nabal similar to his relationship with Saul?

8. What lesson is the Lord repeatedly trying to drive home to David and to us?

9. How would Nabal's fate encourage David to trust God about Saul?

10. Think of someone who has recently mistreated you. How can this study affect your attitude and actions toward that person?

Take time to pray for that person. Ask the Lord for grace to show love toward the person and to entrust the matter into God's hands.

Now or Later

In Romans 12:19-21 Paul writes, "Do not take revenge, my friends, but leave room for God's wrath, for it is written: 'It is mine to avenge; I will repay,' says the Lord. On the contrary: 'If your enemy is hungry, feed him; if he is thirsty, give him something to drink.'" What are some additional ways we can overcome evil with good?

6

Finding Strength
in the Lord

1 Samuel 30:1-25

In a chapter titled "The False Hope of Modern Christianity," Larry Crabb writes, "Modern Christianity, in dramatic reversal of its biblical form, promises to relieve the pain of living in a fallen world. The message, whether it's from fundamentalists requiring us to live by a favored set of rules or from charismatics urging a deeper surrender of the Spirit's power, is too often the same: The promise of bliss is for NOW! Complete satisfaction can be ours this side of Heaven." (*Inside Out* [Colorado Springs, Colo.: NavPress, 1988], p. 15).

GROUP DISCUSSION. The Christian life is often portrayed as a before-and-after story, with everything "after" being sweetness and light. How do you respond to that kind of portrayal?

PERSONAL REFLECTION. In what ways have you struggled or faced difficulties since becoming a Christian?

In this chapter David and his men experience a devastating crisis. Yet in the midst of the crisis, they also find strength and help in the Lord. *Read 1 Samuel 30:1-25.*

---

1. How does the mood of this chapter change from one scene to another?

2. When David and his men return to their home in Ziklag, what do they find (vv. 1-3)?

What are we told about the depths of their distress (vv. 4-6)?

---

3. Think of a time in your life when you felt overwhelmed by a problem. How did you respond—with tears, bitterness or in some other way? Explain.

---

4. In the midst of his distress, how do you think David "found strength in the LORD his God" (v. 6)?

---

5. In what ways can we find strength in the Lord during our times of distress?

---

6. After David has found strength in the Lord, how does he also find help from the Lord (vv. 7-20)?

---

7. What was wrong with the logic of those who said, "Because they did not go out with us, we will not share with them the plunder we recovered" (v. 22)?

8. David declares that the Lord "has protected us and handed over to us the forces that came against us" (v. 23). If the Lord was able to do all that, why do you think he allowed the problem to arise in the first place?

9. How can David's experience help us to have a realistic view of the difficulties we might face as Christians?

10. What difficulty or distress are you currently facing?

How can David's experience give you hope?

Ask God for the strength you need in the midst of your difficulty.

Now or Later

In 2 Corinthians 12:9-10 the Lord says to Paul in the midst of his hardship, "'My grace is sufficient for you, for my power is made perfect in weakness.'" Paul responds, "Therefore I will boast all the more gladly about my weaknesses, so that Christ's power may rest on me. That is why, for Christ's sake, I delight in weaknesses, in insults, in hardships, in persecutions, in difficulties. For when I am weak, then I am strong." How has God's grace been sufficient for you during difficult times? In what ways have you found God's power "made perfect" in your weakness?

7

God's Wrath
& Blessing

2 Samuel 6

In the Chronicles of Narnia we are introduced to Aslan, the son of the great Emperor-Beyond-the Sea, in this way:

> "Don't you know who is the King of Beasts? Aslan is a lion—the Lion, the great Lion."
>
> "Ooh!" said Susan, "I'd thought he was a man. Is he—quite safe? I shall feel rather nervous about meeting a lion."
>
> "That you will, dearie, and no mistake," said Mrs. Beaver. "If there's anyone who can appear before Aslan without their knees knocking, they're either braver than most or else just silly."
>
> "Then he isn't safe?" said Lucy.
>
> "Safe?" said Mr. Beaver. "Don't you hear what Mrs. Beaver tells you? Who said anything about safe? Course he isn't safe. But he's good."

GROUP DISCUSSION. How does Lewis's description of Aslan help you understand what it means to "fear the Lord"?

PERSONAL REFLECTION. Why do God's goodness and his holiness sometimes seem contradictory?

In this chapter David learns in a terrible way that the Lord, the God of Israel, isn't safe. But he also gains a greater appreciation of God's goodness. *Read 2 Samuel 6.*

1. What words would you use to describe the mood of those bringing the ark to Jerusalem (vv. 1-5)?

2. Why do you think David and the people of Israel viewed this as an occasion to celebrate with all their might (v. 5)?

3. Uzzah's act of taking hold of the ark seems well-intentioned (v. 6). Why then did the Lord's anger burn against him (v. 7; see also 1 Chronicles 15:11-15)?

4. Why are sincerity and good intentions sometimes not enough to please the Lord?

5. After Uzzah died, David became both angry and afraid of the Lord (vv. 8-9). How would you evaluate his emotional response?

6. Although the Lord had struck down Uzzah, he blessed the house of Obed-Edom (vv. 10-11). What was the Lord saying about himself through these events?

7. What new precautions does David take as he moves the ark to

Jerusalem (vv. 12-15)?

8. Describe Michal's response in verses 16-20.

Now look at the information in verses 21-23. How would you evaluate her reaction?

9. In what ways was this event marked by celebration (vv. 17-19)?

10. Do your times of worship tend to be somber or joyous? Explain.

11. In what ways can you make your times of worship more of a joyous celebration?

Ask God to give you a fresh vision of his holiness and his goodness.

Now or Later

God's holiness and goodness are most clearly revealed in the cross of Christ. God's holiness demanded the death of his Son for our sins. But his goodness and love flow out from the cross offering us acceptance, forgiveness and eternal life. Take time now to worship God and to thank him for the gift of salvation.

8

God's Promise to David

At some point in our lives, most of us want to do great things for God. We may imagine ourselves as world-famous evangelists, proclaiming the good news to thousands. Or we may aspire to be great Bible expositors, holding people spellbound with our oratory. Or perhaps we will be the next Mother Teresa, bringing care to the sick and needy.

GROUP DISCUSSION. Have you ever wanted to do great things for God? Explain.

PERSONAL REFLECTION. In what ways has God used you to accomplish his purposes?

David wanted to build a magnificent temple for the Lord. However, in this passage he is surprised to discover that God's plans for David are far greater than David's plans for God. *Read 2 Samuel 7.*

1. What different names for God are used in this passage?

2. What prompts David to want to build a house for the Lord (vv. 1-3)?

3. Nathan initially tells David to go ahead with his plan (v. 3). But according to the Lord, what have both Nathan and David failed to take into account (vv.4-7)?

4. Throughout history, sincere people have built monuments for the Lord that he never asked for. How can we avoid involvement in these misguided projects?

5. Verses 8-16 have been called the Davidic covenant. What specific promises does God make to David?

6. Who is the offspring (v. 12) who will build a house for the Lord and whose kingdom God will establish (see 1 Kings 5:1-5; 6:11-13)?

7. How do the promises in verses 8-16 find their ultimate fulfillment in Jesus Christ (see, for example, Luke 1:30-33)?

8. After hearing God's promises to him, David prays (v. 18). Why is he astonished not only with the promises but with God himself (vv. 18-24)?

9. When have you been astonished to discover that both God and his plans are far greater than you imagined?

---

10. After praising God for his greatness, what requests does David make (vv. 25-29)?

---

11. If the "Sovereign LORD" has already guaranteed to fulfill his promises, then why do you think David asks him to do so?

What insights does this give us into the relationship between God's sovereignty and our responsibility?

---

12. In what ways has the Lord demonstrated his greatness or goodness to you recently?

Take time to thank him for all that he has done for you.

Now or Later

David refers to God as "Sovereign LORD" seven times in verses 18-29. In what ways are you trusting in God to accomplish his purposes for your life? David refers to himself ten times as the Lord's "servant" in verses 19-29. Why is this an appropriate way to view yourself in light of God's sovereignty?

9

Facing Temptation

2 Samuel 11

In *Lake Wobegon Days* Garrison Keillor describes a priest named Father Emil, who presides over Our Lady of Perpetual Responsibility Catholic Church. Every year Father Emil faithfully delivers a sermon on the evils of birth control. He titles it "If You Didn't Want to Go to Minneapolis, Why Did You Get on the Train?" His point, of course, is that if we want to avoid certain consequences, we must avoid certain actions.

GROUP DISCUSSION. How do you respond when you hear that a respected Christian leader has committed a serious sin?

PERSONAL REFLECTION. How do the potential consequences of your actions affect your daily behavior?

The story of David and Bathsheba reveals how a series of smaller sins can build to tragic and devastating results. We also discover what forces can lead "a man after God's own heart" to commit adultery and murder. *Read 2 Samuel 11.*

1. Sin often begins with a series of temptations, each one leading to the next. What steps led to David's sin with Bathsheba (vv. 1-5)?

2. At each stage of his temptation, what might David have done to keep from taking the next step? (Be specific.)

3. Why do you think Satan often entices us with a series of temptations rather than offering us one "big" temptation?

4. At what point does a temptation become sin?

5. What plan does David devise to cover up his sin (vv. 6-13)?

How does Uriah thwart David's plan—at least initially?

6. Why are we tempted to cover up our sins rather than to confess them?

7. When deceit fails to work, how does David's plan become vicious (vv. 14-15)?

8. What other people does David draw into the wake of his sin?

9. As you look back over this chapter, how would you explain what led "a man after God's own heart" to commit adultery and murder?

10. In what specific ways can David's experience be a warning to us?

Ask God to guard and protect you from seemingly "small" temptations. Pray that he will enable you to stop the snowballing effect of temptation and sin.

Now or Later

Thomas à Kempis said, "The process works like this. First, the thought is allowed to enter into our minds. Second, the imagination is sparked by the thought. Third, we feel a sense of pleasure at the fantasy, and we entertain it. Fourth and finally, we engage in the evil action, assenting to its urges. This is how, little by little, temptations gain entrance and overcome us if they are not resisted at the beginning. The longer we let them overcome us, the weaker we become, and the stronger the enemy against us" (Quoted in Richard J. Foster and James Bryan Smith, *Devotional Classics* [San Francisco: Harper Collins, 1989], p. 85). How does this quote give you insight into the nature of temptation and sin?

10

God's Severe
Mercy

2 Samuel 12

It often seems easier to cover up our sin than to confess it. When my son, Chris, was about four years old, he decided to do some pruning in our garden. My wife had carefully planted red and yellow tulips, and they were in full bloom. As we went into the garden to admire them, we couldn't believe our eyes. Every petal had been cut off, and all that was left were the tall, naked stems.

"Christopher James!" I cried out. "What did you do to the tulips?"

"Nothing, daddy," he replied.

"Are you sure?" I countered.

"Uh huh."

"Don't lie to me, Chris. I won't punish you if you tell me the truth."

There was a long pause, and then he said, "Even if I *did* it?"

GROUP DISCUSSION. Why are we tempted to cover up our sin rather than to confess it?

PERSONAL REFLECTION. How do you respond when someone confronts you about something you know you've done wrong?

In the previous chapter, David sought desperately to hide what he had done. Then, when David assumes his "problem" is safely behind him,

Nathan appears with a message from God. This chapter gives us a powerful example of God's severe mercy. *Read 2 Samuel 12.*

---

1. Why do you think Nathan tells David a story rather than confronting him directly about his sin?

---

2. Why is it so difficult for us to be objective about our own sin?

---

3. Why is the Lord amazed that David despised both him and his word (vv.7-10)?

---

4. When we sin, how do we display contempt for God and his Word?

---

5. How are God's justice and mercy revealed in his decision about David's sin (vv. 10-14)?

---

6. We normally assume that God disciplines us for our benefit (see Hebrews 12:5-13). Is God's treatment of David an example of beneficial discipline, or is God demanding a penalty for David's sin? Explain.

7. How does David respond to the news that his child is ill (vv. 15-17)?

---

8. How would you evaluate David's method of pleading with the Lord?

---

9. After the child dies, how is God's grace again evident in David's life (vv. 23-25)?

---

10. The author of Hebrews writes: "No discipline seems pleasant at the time, but painful. Later on, however, it produces a harvest of righteousness and peace for those who have been trained by it" (12:11). In what ways has God's painful discipline had that effect in your life?

Take time to thank God for his severe mercy in your life. Ask him for grace to see his love and care in the midst of his discipline.

Now or Later

The author of Hebrews tells us we face two options when God disciplines us. Either we can accept his discipline and be healed, or we can resist his discipline and risk a permanent disability: "Therefore, strengthen your feeble arms and weak knees. 'Make level paths for your feet,' so that the lame may not be disabled, but rather healed" (Hebrews 12:12-13). Think of an area in your life where you are experiencing God's discipline. How can you cooperate with him in that healing process?

11

Misplaced Trust

October 29, 1929, is known as "Black Tuesday," the day of the Wall Street crash and the beginning of the Great Depression. One person wrote, "The thing I remember most about the Depression is my father saying, 'So and so killed himself today.' And I suppose ten of my father's friends committed suicide in the banking business." Over 600,000 homeowners lost their property between 1930 and 1932. More than 5,000 banks failed. Depositors lost a total of $7 billion dollars. By 1933, 25 percent of the work force—nearly 13 million people—did not have jobs.

What makes you feel secure? Is it a steady job? a large savings account? good health? family and friends? Each of these can be a gift from the Lord and a reason for giving thanks. However, when we begin to trust in the gift rather than the Giver, we are headed for trouble.

GROUP DISCUSSION. What sorts of things contribute to your feelings of security?

PERSONAL REFLECTION. In what ways are you tempted to trust in your circumstances rather than in God?

In this chapter David discovers the terrible consequences of misplaced trust. *Read 1 Chronicles 21:1—22:1.*

1. What do you think motivated David to take a census of Israel?

2. In what ways does the author make it clear that David's action was evil?

3. Unfortunately, the author does not tell us why David's action was sinful. Why might the Lord have viewed David's action as sinful?

4. Why are we often tempted to trust in human strength and resources rather than in the Lord?

5. If you were David, which of the three options for punishment would you choose, and why (vv. 11-13)?

6. In what sense was the plague on Israel (v. 14) appropriate to David's sin?

7. What are some of the perils of finding our security in something or someone other than the Lord?

8. What contributes to the mood of fear and urgency in verses 16-27?

9. Why do you think the author devotes half of the chapter to David's purchase of the threshing floor?

10. Why was this an appropriate site for building the house of the Lord (22:1)?

11. Animal sacrifices are no longer necessary to atone for our sins (Hebrews 10:11-12). What then should we do when we discover we are guilty of misplaced trust?

If you are aware of areas of misplaced trust in your life, take time now to confess them to the Lord. Thank him for the forgiveness and security we have in Christ.

Now or Later

Take time to read and meditate on Psalm 37:3-6:

> Trust in the LORD and do good;
>   dwell in the land and enjoy safe pasture.
> Delight yourself in the LORD
>   and he will give you the desires of your heart.
>
> Commit your way to the LORD;
>   trust in him and he will do this:
> He will make your righteousness shine like the dawn,
>   the justice of your cause like the noonday sun.

12

Generous Giving

1 Chronicles 29

Giving has become a sore spot for many Christians. Every day we are bombarded with appeals for money—from television and radio evangelists, from missionaries, from parachurch organizations, from telephone solicitors and from our own churches. Sometimes we feel like shouting, "Enough is enough!" How can we adopt godly attitudes toward giving so that we don't live with a closed fist but an open hand and a generous heart?

GROUP DISCUSSION. How do you tend to respond when people ask you for money? Explain.

PERSONAL REFLECTION. How would you describe your own attitude toward giving?

David had a refreshing attitude toward giving. In this chapter he illustrates what it means to give joyously and generously to the Lord. *Read 1 Chronicles 29.*

1. What does this chapter reveal about David's perspective on giving?

2. How does David provide an excellent example of what it means to give generously to God (vv. 1-5)?

_____

3. What effect does David's example have on the leaders of Israel and the people (vv. 6-9)?

_____

4. In what ways have you been motivated to give more generously or to dedicate yourself more fully by observing the personal example of Christian leaders?

_____

5. What does David's prayer in verses 10-13 reveal about his view of God?

_____

6. How is our view of God related to our willingness or unwillingness to give generously?

7. David might have felt boastful about his giving. What do verses 14-19 reveal about his reasons for humility?

———————————————————————————————

8. David might also have felt remorse about parting with so much of his wealth. Instead, what spiritual and emotional impact did it have on him and the people (vv. 20-25)?

———————————————————————————————

9. According to this chapter, in what other ways can we express our devotion to the Lord?

———————————————————————————————

10. Verses 26-30 record the death of David. How do the events in this chapter provide a fitting conclusion to his life?

———————————————————————————————

11. What have you appreciated most about studying the life of David?

12. In what ways have you been challenged by his example?

Thank the Lord for David's example. Pray that you, like David, will develop a passionate heart for God.

Now or Later

Take a personal inventory of your resources. Write down specific ways you could give more generously in the following areas:

Your time:

Your talents:

Your money:

Leader's Notes

MY GRACE IS SUFFICIENT FOR YOU. (2 COR 12:9)

Leading a Bible discussion can be an enjoyable and rewarding experience. But it can also be *scary*—especially if you've never done it before. If this is your feeling, you're in good company. When God asked Moses to lead the Israelites out of Egypt, he replied, "O Lord, please send someone else to do it"! (Ex 4:13). It was the same with Solomon, Jeremiah and Timothy, but God helped these people in spite of their weaknesses, and he will help you as well.

You don't need to be an expert on the Bible or a trained teacher to lead a Bible discussion. The idea behind these inductive studies is that the leader guides group members to discover for themselves what the Bible has to say. This method of learning will allow group members to remember much more of what is said than a lecture would.

These studies are designed to be led easily. As a matter of fact, the flow of questions through the passage from observation to interpretation to application is so natural that you may feel that the studies lead themselves. This study guide is also flexible. You can use it with a variety of groups—student, professional, neighborhood or church groups. Each study takes forty-five to sixty minutes in a group setting.

There are some important facts to know about group dynamics and encouraging discussion. The suggestions listed below should enable you to effectively and enjoyably fulfill your role as leader.

Preparing for the Study

1. Ask God to help you understand and apply the passage in your own life. Unless this happens, you will not be prepared to lead others. Pray too for the various members of the group. Ask God to open your hearts to the message of his Word and motivate you to action.

2. Read the introduction to the entire guide to get an overview of the entire book and the issues which will be explored.

3. As you begin each study, read and reread the assigned Bible passage to familiarize yourself with it.

4. This study guide is based on the New International Version of the Bible. It will help you and the group if you use this translation as the basis for your study and discussion.

5. Carefully work through each question in the study. Spend time in meditation and reflection as you consider how to respond.

6. Write your thoughts and responses in the space provided in the study guide. This will help you to express your understanding of the passage clearly.

7. It might help to have a Bible dictionary handy. Use it to look up any unfamiliar words, names or places. (For additional help on how to study a passage, see chapter five of *How to Lead a LifeBuilder Study*, IVP, 2018.)

8. Consider how you can apply the Scripture to your life. Remember that the group will follow your lead in responding to the studies. They will not go any deeper than you do.

9. Once you have finished your own study of the passage, familiarize yourself with the leader's notes for the study you are leading. These are designed to help you in several ways. First, they tell you the purpose the study guide author had in mind when writing the study. Take time to think through how the study questions work together to accomplish that purpose. Second, the notes provide you with additional background information or suggestions on group dynamics for various questions. This information can be useful when people have difficulty understanding or answering a question. Third, the leader's notes can alert you to potential problems you may encounter during the study.

10. If you wish to remind yourself of anything mentioned in the leader's notes, make a note to yourself below that question in the study.

Leading the Study

1. Begin the study on time. Open with prayer, asking God to help the group to understand and apply the passage.

2. Be sure that everyone in your group has a study guide. Encourage the group to prepare beforehand for each discussion by reading the introduction to the guide and by working through the questions in the study.

3. At the beginning of your first time together, explain that these studies are meant to be discussions, not lectures. Encourage the members of the group to participate. However, do not put pressure on those who may be hesitant to speak during the first few sessions. You may want to suggest the following guidelines to your group.

☐ Stick to the topic being discussed.

☐ Your responses should be based on the verses which are the focus of the discussion and not on outside authorities such as commentaries or speakers.

☐ These studies focus on a particular passage of Scripture. Only rarely should you refer to other portions of the Bible. This allows for everyone to participate in in-depth study on equal ground.

☐ Anything said in the group is considered confidential and will not be discussed outside the group unless specific permission is given to do so.

☐ We will listen attentively to each other and provide time for each person present to talk.

☐ We will pray for each other.

4. Have a group member read the introduction at the beginning of the discussion.

5. Every session begins with a group discussion question. The question or activity is meant to be used before the passage is read. The question introduces the theme of the study and encourages group members to begin to open up. Encourage as many members as possible to participate, and be ready to get the discussion going with your own response.

This section is designed to reveal where our thoughts or feelings need to be transformed by Scripture. That is why it is especially important not to read the passage before the discussion question is asked. The passage will tend to color the honest reactions people would otherwise give because they are, of course, supposed to think the way the Bible does.

You may want to supplement the group discussion question with an icebreaker to help people to get comfortable. See the community section of the *Small Group Starter Kit* (IVP, 1995) for more ideas.

You also might want to use the personal reflection question with your group. Either allow a time of silence for people to respond individually or discuss it together.

6. Have a group member (or members if the passage is long) read aloud the passage to be studied. Then give people several minutes to read the passage again silently so that they can take it all in.

7. Question 1 will generally be an overview question designed to briefly survey the passage. Encourage the group to look at the whole passage, but try to avoid getting sidetracked by questions or issues that will be addressed later in the study.

8. As you ask the questions, keep in mind that they are designed to be used just as they are written. You may simply read them aloud. Or you may prefer to express them in your own words.

There may be times when it is appropriate to deviate from the study guide. For example, a question may have already been answered. If so, move on to the next question. Or someone may raise an important question not covered in the guide. Take time to discuss it, but try to keep the group from going off on tangents.

9. Avoid answering your own questions. If necessary, repeat or rephrase them until they are clearly understood. Or point out something you read in the leader's notes to clarify the context or meaning. An eager group quickly becomes passive and silent if they think the leader will do most of the talking.

10. Don't be afraid of silence. People may need time to think about the question before formulating their answers.

11. Don't be content with just one answer. Ask, "What do the rest of you think?" or "Anything else?" until several people have given answers to the question.

12. Acknowledge all contributions. Try to be affirming whenever possible. Never reject an answer. If it is clearly off-base, ask, "Which verse led you to that conclusion?" or again, "What do the rest of you think?"

13. Don't expect every answer to be addressed to you, even though this will probably happen at first. As group members become more at ease, they will begin to truly interact with each other. This is one sign of healthy discussion.

14. Don't be afraid of controversy. It can be very stimulating. If you don't resolve an issue completely, don't be frustrated. Move on and keep it in mind for later. A subsequent study may solve the problem.

15. Periodically summarize what the group has said about the passage. This helps to draw together the various ideas mentioned and gives continuity to the study. But don't preach.

16. At the end of the Bible discussion you may want to allow group members a time of quiet to work on an idea under "Now or Later." Then discuss what you experienced. Or you may want to encourage group members to work on these ideas between meetings. Give an opportunity during the session for people to talk about what they are learning.

17. Conclude your time together with conversational prayer, adapting the prayer suggestion at the end of the study to your group. Ask for God's help in following through on the commitments you've made.

18. End on time.

Many more suggestions and helps are found in *How to Lead a LifeBuilder Study*.

Components of Small Groups

A healthy small group should do more than study the Bible. There are four components to consider as you structure your time together.

Nurture. Small groups help us to grow in our knowledge and love of God. Bible study is the key to making this happen and is the foundation of your small group.

Community. Small groups are a great place to develop deep friendships with other Christians. Allow time for informal interaction before and after each study. Plan activities and games that will help you get to know each other. Spend time having fun together—going on a picnic or cooking dinner together.

Worship and prayer. Your study will be enhanced by spending time praising God together in prayer or song. Pray for each other's needs—and keep track of how God is answering prayer in your group. Ask God to help you to apply what you are learning in your study.

Outreach. Reaching out to others can be a practical way of applying what you are learning, and it will keep your group from becoming self-focused. Host a series of evangelistic discussions for your friends or neighbors. Clean up the yard of an elderly friend. Serve at a soup kitchen together, or spend a day working in the community.

Many more suggestions and helps in each of these areas are found in the *Small Group Starter Kit*. You will also find information on building a small group. Reading through the starter kit will be worth your time.

Study 1. The Lord Looks at the Heart.
1 Samuel 16:1-13.

Purpose: To contrast our typical way of looking at people with the Lord's way.

Question 1. "This chapter begins where chapter 15 ends: Samuel is still mourning for Saul. Ironically, the divine 'how long' serves as a prophetic rebuke to the prophet Samuel. Since God had rejected Saul as king over Israel, a change of leadership was in order" (*NIV Bible Commentary*, eds. Kenneth Barker & John Kohlenberger [Grand Rapids: Zondervan, 1994], p. 53).

Question 3. Not only was Eliab tall and handsome, he was also Jesse's firstborn son (1 Sam 17:13), the one who normally would have been chosen first in Israel's culture.

Question 5. Encourage the group to explore not only outward appearance—height, beauty, clothes and so on—but also other external qualities such as position, education or influence.

Question 7. You might ask the group to think of people they know or have known whose inner qualities and abilities far exceeded what their meek exterior might suggest.

Question 9. It is interesting that the Lord didn't simply tell Samuel that David was the one he should anoint. Instead, he allowed Samuel to go through the entire family before coming to David. Initially, Samuel used worldly criteria in supposing that Eliab was the Lord's anointed. Yet as he went down the line of Jesse's sons, the truth began to sink in that "the Lord does not look at the things man looks at. Man looks at the outward appearance, but the Lord looks at the heart." The process was an educational experience for Samuel and everyone else in David's family.

Study 2. The Battle Is the Lord's. 1 Samuel 17.
Purpose: To realize that "it is not by sword or spear that the LORD saves; for the battle is the LORD's" (1 Sam 17:47).

Question 1. In ancient times, battles were sometimes fought not by entire armies but by champions chosen to represent them. As the champions fought, the gods supposedly decided the outcome of the battle. The Philistines evidently believed in this practice and chose Goliath as their champion.

From a human standpoint, Goliath was awesome. The text tells us that he was over nine feet tall (v. 4). His armor of bronze weighed about 125 pounds (about 57 kilograms), and the iron point of his spear weighed about 15 pounds (about 7 kilograms). In addition, he had been a fighting man since his youth (v. 33). He was the ideal warrior, and Israel had good reason to be afraid of him.

Question 2. In Deuteronomy 20:1-4 God had promised: "When you go to war against your enemies and see horses and chariots and an army greater than yours, do not be afraid of them, because the LORD your God, who brought you up out of Egypt, will be with you. When you are about to go into battle, the priest shall come forward and address the army. He shall say: 'Hear, O Israel, today you are going into battle against your enemies. Do not be fainthearted or afraid; do not be terrified or give way to panic before them. For the LORD your God is the one who goes with you to fight for you against your enemies to give you victory.'" The actions of Saul and the Israelites revealed a lack of faith in God's promises. The Lord had promised to fight for them and give them victory, regardless of the size of the army they faced.

Question 3. If you feel you have time, at this point you might add the question, What promises do we need to remember during the battles of life? Then have four volunteers read the following passages: Matthew 28:20, Romans 8:28, 2 Corinthians 12:9, Hebrews 13:5-6. Others may also be able to recall promises that have helped them in life's battles.

Question 5. The author of 1 Samuel goes to great lengths in this chapter to emphasize what a mismatch this battle was, at least from a human standpoint. David's weakness forms a backdrop for displaying the Lord's power.

Saul was risking the entire future of Israel by allowing David to go into battle. If David had lost, Israel would have become the slaves of the Philistines (see note to question 2).

Question 7. David isn't boasting about his own abilities or victories. In verse 37 he reveals that the Lord delivered him in the past and expresses faith that the Lord will likewise deliver him in his battle with Goliath.

Question 9. Verse 47 presents the main message of this chapter: "All those gathered here will know that it is not by sword or spear that the LORD saves; for the battle is the LORD's, and he will give all of you into our hands."

Study 3. True Friendship. 1 Samuel 20:1-17, 30-42.
Purpose: To learn something about true friendship through observing David's relationship with Jonathan.

Question 2. Jonathan could have been intimidated by David. Normally, Jonathan would have been the successor to Saul as king of Israel. Yet even when it became clear that David would eventually become king, Jonathan's love persisted.

Question 4. Jonathan's love for David resulted in his being alienated from his father. Jonathan also risked his life by defending David. The *Zondervan NIV*

Bible Commentary states: "As David had feared (v. 7), Saul became violently angry when Jonathan told him the reason for David's absence. For all intents and purposes, Jonathan and David were indistinguishable to Saul as he exploded. Saul curses Jonathan by a vile epithet hurled at his son. He accuses Jonathan of having 'sided with' David, and that not only to his own shame but also the shame of the 'mother who bore you.' Saul further reminded Jonathan that so long as David remained alive, neither Jonathan nor Jonathan's kingdom could survive. History would prove Saul's fears to be prophetic beyond his worst nightmares: although the kingdom of Saul and his son would not be established (1 Sam 13:13-14), the kingdom of David and his son would be (2 Sam 7:16, 26; 1 Kings 2:12, 46)" (*Zondervan NIV Bible Commentary*, eds., Kenneth L. Barker & John Kohlenberger III, [Grand Rapids, Mich.: Zondervan, 1994], 1: 416-17.)

Question 6. According to 1 Samuel 20:41, these two warriors did not consider it "unmanly" to express both physical and emotional love for each other. (Physical affection between men is much more common in Eastern culture than it is in the West.) They also reiterated their commitment to remain friends (v. 42).

Study 4. A Matter of Conscience. 1 Samuel 24.

Purpose: To reexamine some of our notions about guidance.

Question 2. Everything seemed to indicate that it was God's will for David to kill Saul. The Lord had delivered Saul into David's hands (v.10); David's men all agreed that killing Saul was the right thing for David to do; and David even had a specific promise that "I will give your enemy into your hands for you to deal with as you wish" (v. 4). With such seemingly overwhelming evidence, it is remarkable that David refused to kill Saul.

Questions 4 & 6. Two additional factors convinced David that he should not harm Saul: first, he was conscience-stricken after cutting the corner off Saul's robe; second, he recognized that Saul was still the Lord's anointed and, therefore, David's master. David realized that the Lord had anointed Saul, and therefore it was the Lord's responsibility—not David's—to remove Saul from the throne.

Question 9. David still had many lessons to learn about God before he would be ready to sit on the throne of Israel. If he had avoided that long, difficult process of maturity, he would not have been the kind of king he eventually became. Likewise, if he had shown contempt for the Lord's anointed by killing him and seizing his throne, then how would others have treated David when he became recognized as God's anointed?

Study 5. Secure in the Lord. 1 Samuel 25.

Purpose: To consider both a positive and negative example of how we should respond to those who mistreat us.

Question 1. In the previous chapter and in the one following, David refuses to avenge himself, leaving vengeance in the hands of the Lord. In this chapter he comes very close to exacting his own vengeance against Nabal.

Question 2. In Hebrew the name Nabal means "fool." This account reveals what his wife later declares, that "he is just like his name—his name is Fool" (v. 25).

Question 3. Sheep-shearing time was a festive occasion. Because he had protected Nabal's shepherds and flocks, David had reason to expect some remuneration. However, in anger he overreacts to Nabal's rude response.

Question 7. "Nabal's general character, his disdainful attitude toward David though David had guarded his flocks, and his sudden death at the Lord's hand all parallel Saul (whose 'flock' David had also protected). This allows the author indirectly to characterize Saul as a fool (see 13:13; 26:21) and to foreshadow his end" (*NIV Study Bible,* ed. Kenneth Barker [Grand Rapids, Mich.: Zondervan, 1985], p. 411).

Question 8. David needed reassurance that the Lord would eventually execute vengeance against Saul for the way he treated David, just as the Lord had executed his vengeance against Nabal. Without this reassurance, David would be tempted to avenge himself against Saul. We too need to trust God to deal with our enemies, rather than seeking revenge or ways to get even.

Study 6. Finding Strength in the Lord. 1 Samuel 30:1-25.

Purpose: To encourage us to find strength in the Lord in the midst of our difficulties.

Question 2. David was given the city of Ziklag by Achish, king of Gath, while David lived among the Philistines (see 1 Sam 27:6-7).

Question 6. In verses 7-8 David asks Abiathar the priest to bring him the ephod so that he can inquire of the Lord. The ephod was a special linen garment worn by the high priest. The breastplate attached to the ephod contained two sacred lots, known as the Urim and the Thummim ("the curses and the perfections") which were used during times of crisis to determine the will of God. Presumably, the Urim indicated that the answer was no, and the Thummim indicated that it was yes. However, it is interesting that the Lord's answer to David is not a simple yes, as might be expected, but rather the more detailed response: "Pursue them. You will certainly overtake them and succeed in the rescue" (v. 8).

Question 7. Those who made this claim put special emphasis on their own accomplishments—"the plunder we recovered." In contrast, David attributed their victory to the Lord ("No, my brothers, you must not do that with what the LORD has given us," v. 23). Because the Lord had given them the victory, everyone deserved a share in the plunder.

Question 8. In the final analysis, this question is unanswerable. However, because we regularly face difficulties in a fallen world, it is important to wrestle with the question. It is clear from Scripture that the Lord's children are not exempt from hardships and trials. Yet God gives us grace during those trials and sometimes—but not always—delivers us from them.

Question 10. If the members of your group are threatened by this question, you might rephrase it as follows: "Reflect on a difficulty or distress you are currently facing. How can David's experience give you hope?"

Study 7. God's Wrath & Blessing. 2 Samuel 6.
Purpose: To gain a greater appreciation of God's holiness.
General note. Before reading this chapter you might mention to the group that David is now king over Israel as well as Judah (see 2 Sam 5).
Question 1. In placing the ark on a new cart, David was following the practice of the Philistines (1 Sam 6:7) rather than the method commanded by the Lord (see note to question 3).
Question 3. The ark was not to be moved by placing it in a cart but rather was to be suspended between two long poles and carried on the shoulders of the Levites (1 Chron 15:14-15). Either David was ignorant of Moses' command or he ignored it. Either way, the consequences were severe.
Questions 5-6. The Lord had given David a serious reminder that he is a holy God who demands to be obeyed. However, David's fear was an overreaction. The Lord wanted to bless David and Israel, as is evident from his treatment of Obed-Edom. The problem lay not in trying to bring the ark to Jerusalem but in bringing it in the wrong way.
Question 7. This time David was taking no chances! Not only did he have the Levites carry the ark (see 1 Chron 15) as Moses required, he also offered

sacrifices after six steps—something Moses did not require. However, David's sacrifices may have been offered out of gratitude rather than fear.

Question 8. A few bits of information will help you to navigate these questions: (1) The ephod (v. 14) was a sleeveless pullover, hip length. (2) Verse 16 reveals that Michal "had no appreciation for the significance of the event and deeply resented David's public display as unworthy of the dignity of a king (*NIV Study Bible*, p. 428). (3) Verse 23 may indicate that Michal did not have children as "a punishment for her pride and at the same time another manifestation of God's judgment on the house of Saul" (Ibid.).

Questions 10-11. Consider not only your times of individual worship but also your times of corporate worship, either as a small group or in church.

Study 8. God's Promise to David. 2 Samuel 7.

Purpose: To realize that God's plans for blessing us far exceed our plans for serving him.

Question 2. Because David now lived in a palace (v. 1), he did not think it was appropriate for the heavenly King to dwell in a tent. Therefore, David wanted to build a palace (temple) for the Lord.

Question 3. Both Nathan and David had failed to consult the Lord about building a temple. When the Lord speaks to Nathan, he makes it clear that throughout Israel's history he had never lived in a house and had never asked for one.

Question 5. The Davidic covenant contained the following promises: (1) The Lord would make David's name great (v. 9); (2) the Lord would provide a permanent place for his people (v. 10); (3) they would have rest from all their enemies (v. 11); (4) the Lord would raise up an offspring from David who would build a house for the Lord (vv. 12-13); (5) David's dynasty (house) and kingdom would endure forever (v. 16). This covenant, like those with Noah and Abram, was unconditional.

Questions 6-7. The immediate reference is to Solomon. However, it is also a promise to those descendants of David who would sit on his throne. Ultimately, the promise found its fulfillment in Jesus Christ, the son of David who will rule on David's throne forever (see Mt 1:1; Heb 1:5).

Question 11. "The NIV translates *adonay yahweh* as 'Sovereign LORD.' The first word is an intensive form of 'master' or 'lord' and is used only of God. The second is the personal name of God, indicated in English versions by LORD. Older versions render the phrase by 'LORD God.' The NIV translators chose the word 'sovereign' to represent in English what Hebrew readers would have understood—that the name acknowledges Israel's God as ultimate Lord" (Lawrence O. Richards, *New International Encyclopedia of Bible Words* [Grand Rapids, Mich.: Zondervan, 1999], on CD-ROM.

Study 9. Facing Temptation. 2 Samuel 11.

Purpose: To observe the subtle workings of temptation and how one sin can lead to another so that we can guard ourselves from following David's downward spiral of sin.

Questions 1-2. The author mentions that David's sin happened in the spring, when kings go off to war (v. 1). He points out, however, that David remained in Jerusalem. The impression is given that David's first mistake was to stay home when he should have been out leading his army.

As far as we know, there was nothing wrong with David walking around on the roof of his palace. Likewise, his first glance at Bathsheba might have been unintentional. However, Martin Luther once commented that although we can't keep the birds from flying over our heads, we can keep them from building a nest in our hair!

Next, David inquired about Bathsheba (v. 3). When he found out that she was married to one of his soldiers, David could have dropped the matter. Unfortunately, he had allowed the temptation to gain too much strength to easily be resisted at that point.

Finally, David sent for Bathsheba (v. 4). James helps us understand the process by which temptation becomes sin: "Each one is tempted when, by his own evil desire, he is dragged away and enticed. Then, after desire has conceived, it gives birth to sin; and sin, when it is full-grown, gives birth to death" (Jas 1:14-15). His words could be an apt summary of 2 Samuel 11.

See Leviticus 15:19 and 28 about the parenthetical statement in 2 Samuel 11:4: "She had purified herself from her uncleanness." Verses 4-5 are the author's way of assuring us that Bathsheba was not pregnant prior to sleeping with David.

Question 3. Temptation is usually easier to resist when we are first confronted by it. The longer we allow ourselves to be tempted, the weaker our defenses become. Eventually, we are so strongly under the spell of temptation that we have great difficulty resisting. Satan knows that if he can gradually erode our defenses he will have an easier time getting us to sin.

Question 8. David's sin affects a number of people. Obviously, Bathsheba and

Uriah are affected. Joab's integrity is also compromised. Several other soldiers are killed unnecessarily when they are sent with Uriah on a suicide mission. The pagan nations surrounding Israel feel the impact of David's sin: "By doing this you have made the enemies of the LORD show utter contempt" (2 Sam 12:14). Finally, as we discover in the next chapter, the innocent child is affected by this tragic union.

Question 10. The following saying has always been a warning to me:

Sow a thought, reap an action.

Sow an action, reap a habit.

Sow a habit, reap a character.

Sow a character, reap a destiny.

Study 10. God's Severe Mercy. 2 Samuel 12.

Purpose: To observe God's severe and merciful discipline in the life of David. To consider how and why God disciplines us today.

Question 1. If Nathan had confronted David directly, he would have become defensive. By telling David a story, Nathan allowed David to be more objective and to condemn himself.

It is fitting that Nathan chose a story about a lamb. Perhaps he was hoping to draw out some of the warmth of David's youth, when he was a shepherd who cared for his sheep.

Question 4. You might point out the parallels between our situation and David's. God had given David everything he ever wanted—and more. Yet David repaid God's kindness by committing murder and adultery. Likewise, God gave his Son to die for us when we were helpless and without hope. Now that we are his children, God gives us every spiritual blessing in Christ and lavishly pours out his grace upon us. Whenever we sin, we turn our backs on the One who has loved us to the limit.

Question 5. God's judgment of David seems to be severe. However, we must not overlook the fact that the penalty for adultery and murder should have been death. David had no right to live but was graciously spared by the Lord.

Question 6. There may not be a clear-cut answer to this question. You might point out that when God disciplines us today, that discipline is never an expression of his wrath. Why? Because all the punishment we deserve has already been poured out on Jesus Christ. Instead, our heavenly Father lovingly disciplines us for our good, so that we can share in his holiness. However, because David lived during the old covenant, the issues are not as clear.

Question 9. David's statement, "I will go to him," (v. 23) seems to express his hope in life after death. You may wish to discuss how such a view can help us during a time of bereavement.

It is amazing that the Lord not only gave David and Bathsheba a son to replace the one who had died but also that the son was none other than Solomon, the one God had promised in 2 Samuel 7. The author tells us that the Lord loved Solomon and gave him the name Jedidiah, which means "loved by the LORD" (vv. 24-25). Notice too that the Lord continued to give David victory over his enemies (vv. 26-31).

Question 10. God disciplines us in a variety of ways—not just when we sin, but because we are *sinners* who need to become holy and children who need to grow up.

Study 11. Misplaced Trust. 1 Chronicles 21:1—22:1.
Purpose: To learn to trust in the Lord rather than in human strength and resources.

Question 2. Verse 1 tells us that Satan incited David to take the census. The author mentions that even Joab realized that David's action would bring guilt on Israel (v. 3). Verse 7 states that "this command was also evil in the sight of God." Finally, David himself admitted that he had sinned greatly by taking the census. The author thus leaves no doubt about David's guilt.

Question 3. It may be that David's action was motivated by sinful pride. In addition, it is likely that he was placing his trust in the might of his army rather than in the Lord.

Question 4. This is a strong temptation in our culture. We are inclined to place our trust in our abilities, education or experience, the level of our income, the size of our savings account, or in any number of other visible, tangible things or people. Like David, we need to learn that such things can be taken away in a moment and that our only lasting security is in the Lord.

Question 5. David had numbered his fighting men in order to feel secure against attack. As a result of his sin, seventy thousand men in Israel fell in three days—far more than would have been lost in battle, especially since the Lord would have been fighting for Israel.

Second Samuel 24:1 states that "the anger of the LORD burned against Israel, and he incited David against them saying, 'Go and take a census of Israel and Judah.'" Therefore, the punishment of the people was not solely because of David's sin.

Question 9. One of the author's clear purposes in this chapter is to explain how the site of the temple was acquired (see 22:1).

Question 10. The threshing floor of Araunah the Jebusite was the place where God's wrath was averted from his people through the offer of sacrifice. One of the primary purposes of the temple would be to offer sacrifices for the sins of the people.

Question 11. Like David, we should confess our sins to the Lord, claiming the forgiveness offered through Jesus Christ's death on the cross. Then we should commit our feelings of insecurity to the Lord, asking him to take care of the need that is worrying us. It is also helpful to read about God's past faithfulness in Scripture. David himself provides an excellent summary of God's faithfulness to him in 2 Samuel 22. We might even compose our own psalm of praise, recalling the various ways in which the Lord has provided for our needs, both past and present.

Study 12. Generous Giving. 1 Chronicles 29.

Purpose: To observe through David's example what it means to give joyously and generously to the Lord.

Question 2. The Lord is more concerned about the attitude of our hearts in giving than in the amount. However, it is interesting to note how much David gave to the Lord. From his personal treasure, he gave three thousand talents of gold, which is equivalent to 110 tons (about 100 metric tons). Likewise, he gave seven thousand talents of refined silver, which is equivalent to 260 tons (about 240 metric tons). In today's market value for gold and silver, the monetary value would be staggering.

Questions 5-7. At a moment when David might have felt boastful, we note instead a profound humility. Throughout his prayer, he acknowledges that the Lord already owns everything and that any wealth or honor David possesses are because of God's gift to him (vv. 11-12, 14, 16). David also realizes that our life and wealth are transitory, "like a shadow" (v. 15).

The personal applications are clear. If we realize that the Lord already owns everything, then we will be more humble in our giving. If we realize that the Lord is the source of our wealth, we will be more generous in our giving. Finally, if we, like David, grasp the greatness of God, we will be motivated to worship him through our giving.

Question 9. In addition to giving, this chapter records that David and the people worshiped the Lord through prayer (vv. 10-19), praise (v. 20) and joyous celebration and feasting (v. 22). Although we no longer need to offer animal sacrifices as they did (v. 21), we can worship the Lord through remembering Christ's sacrifice on the cross.

Jack Kuhatschek was formerly executive vice president and publisher at Baker Publishing Group. He is the author of many Bible study guides including Galatians *and* Romans *in the LifeBuilder Bible Study series, and the books* Applying the Bible *and* The Superman Syndrome.